From: Edee on Christmas
Dec. 25, 1967

W9-BVC-725

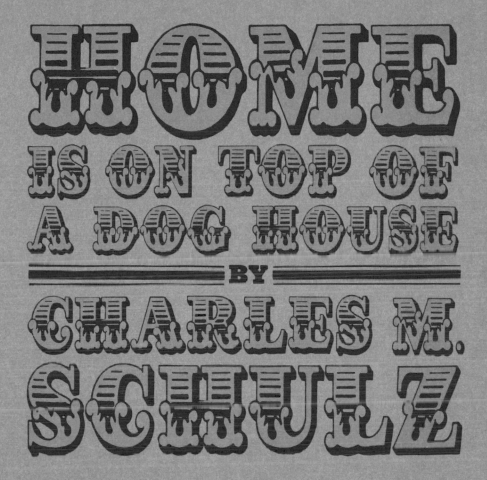

HOME IS ON TOP OF A DOG HOUSE

BY

CHARLES M. SCHULZ

COPYRIGHT 1966
BY UNITED FEATURE
SYNDICATE, INC.

※

PUBLISHED BY
DETERMINED
PRODUCTIONS, INC.
BOX 2150 · SAN FRANCISCO
CALIFORNIA 94126

※

PROJECT DIRECTOR
CONNIE BOUCHER

※

BOOK DESIGN BY
JIM YOUNG

uter

space

fascinates

me.

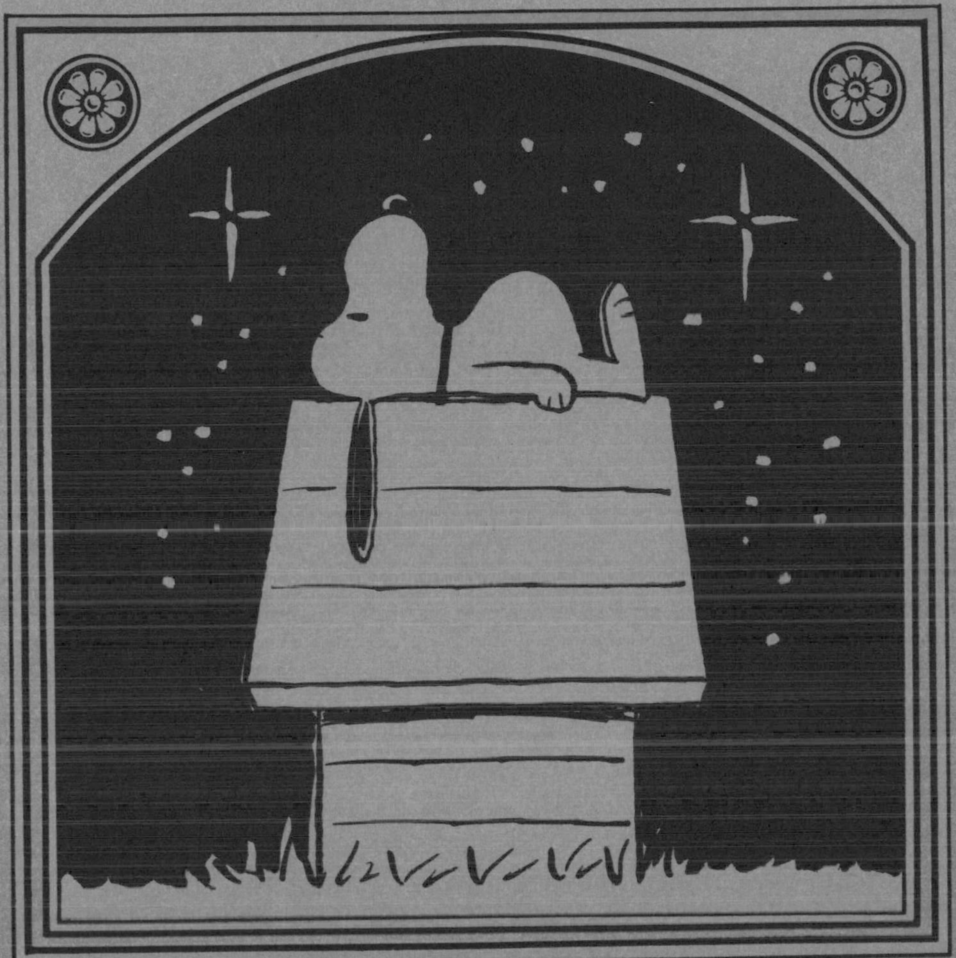

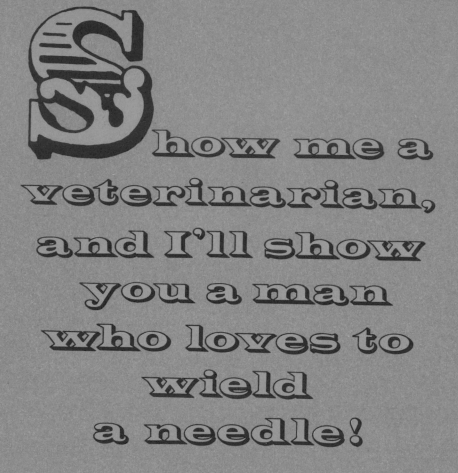

Show me a veterinarian, and I'll show you a man who loves to wield a needle!

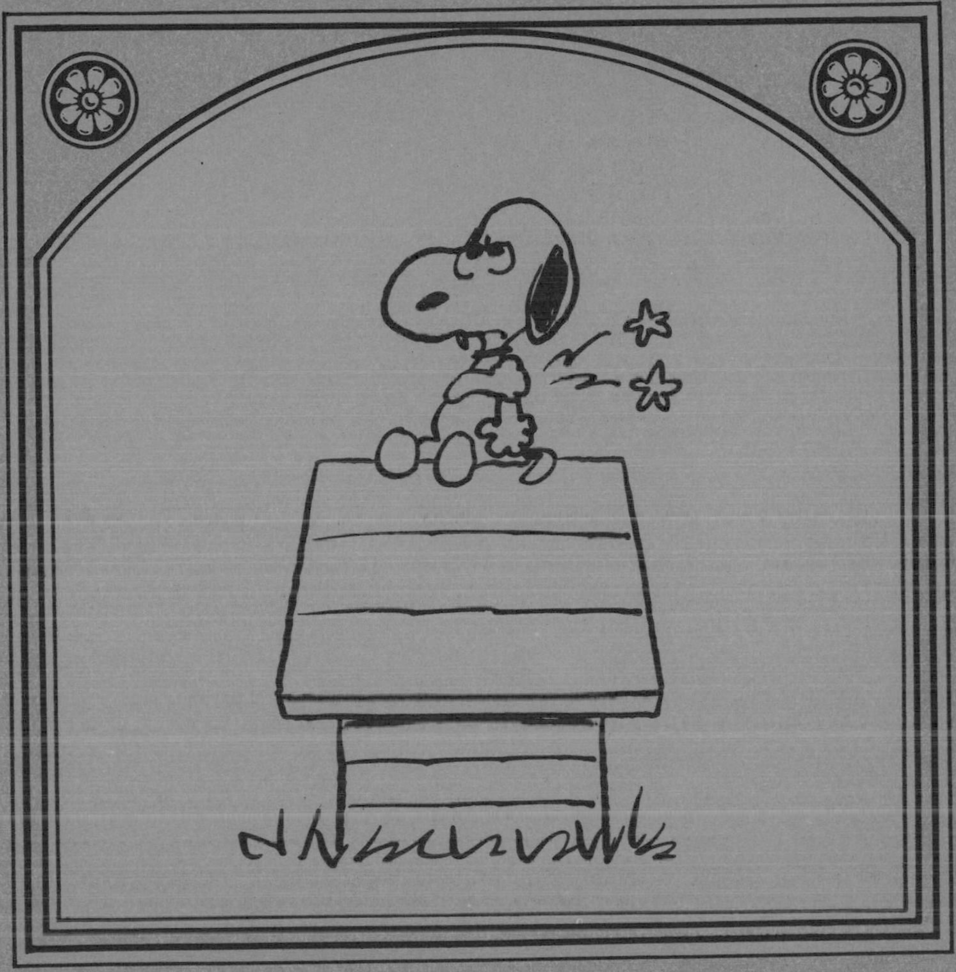

I love to hear the patter of rain on the roof while I'm sleeping.

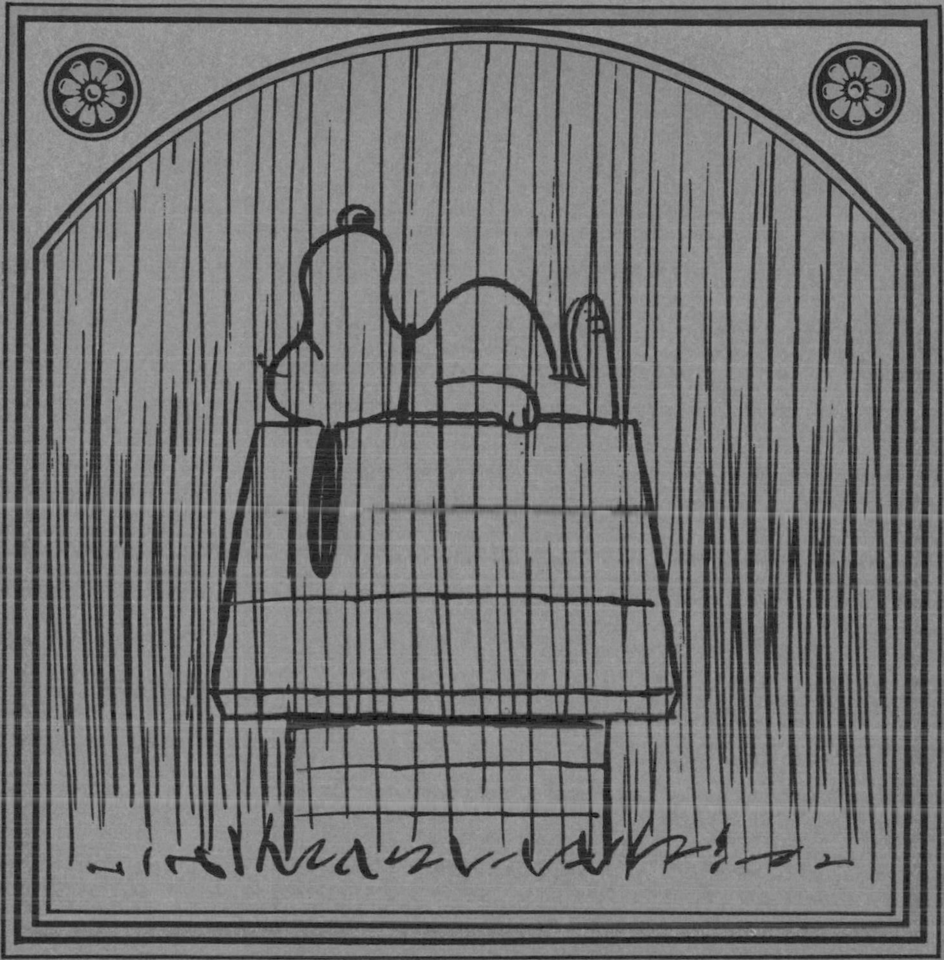

Snow
is
nice
too.

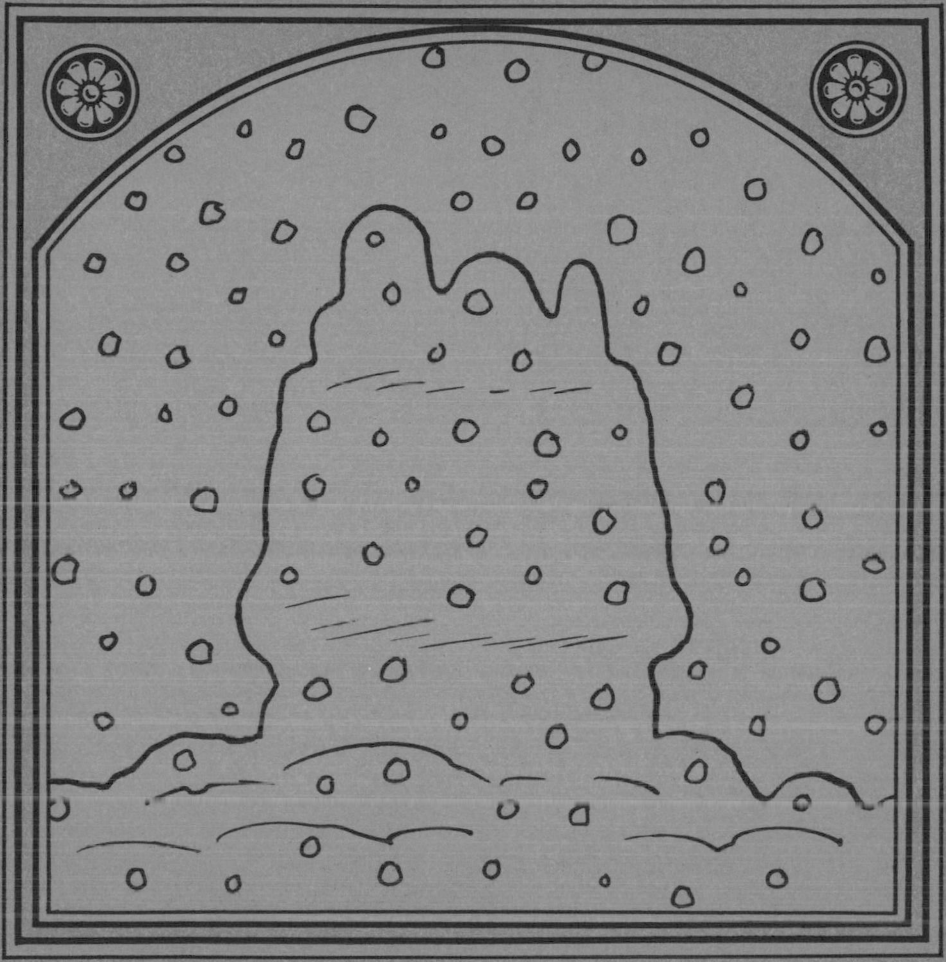

There's the ugliest sight in the world...an empty dog dish!

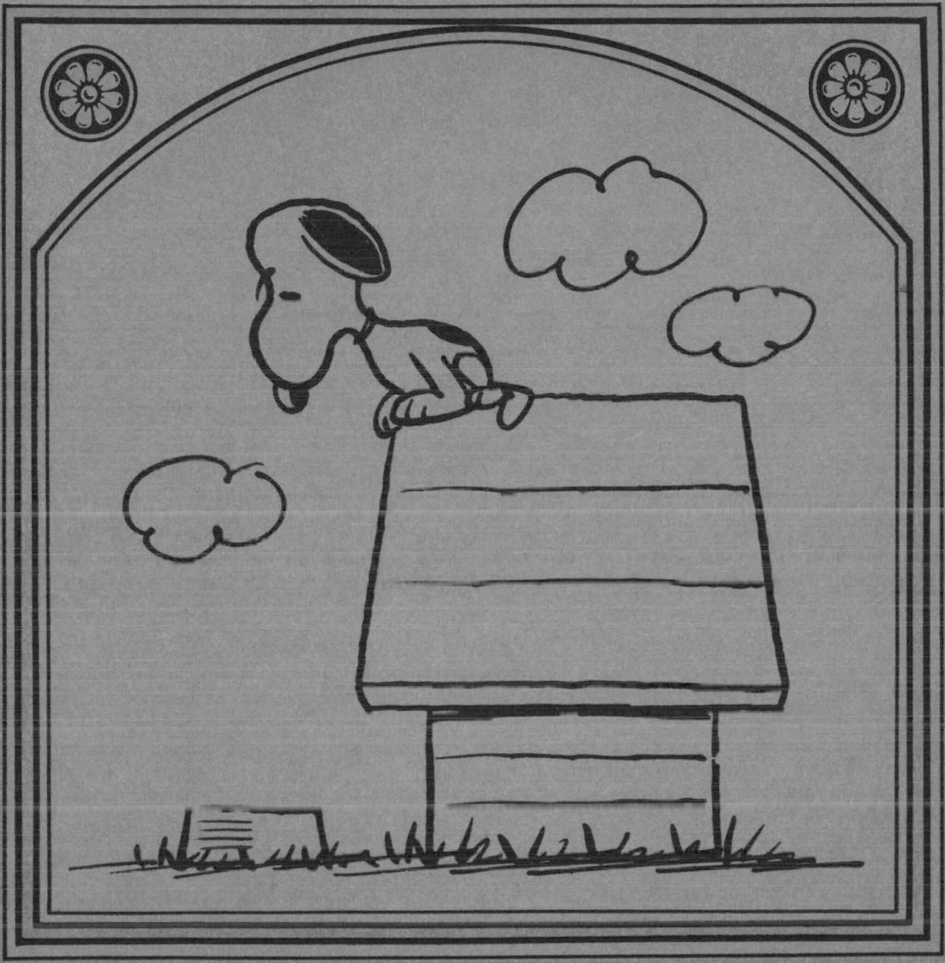

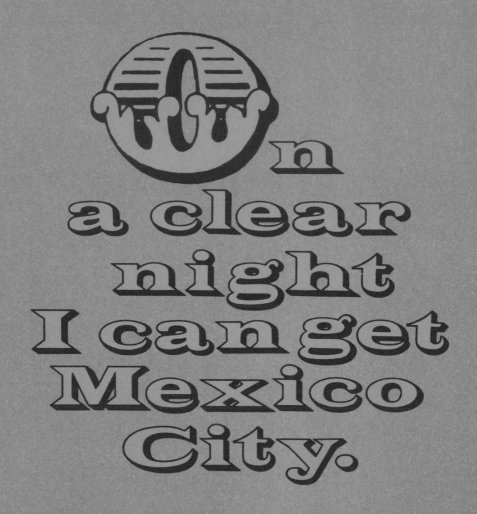

On a clear night I can get Mexico City.

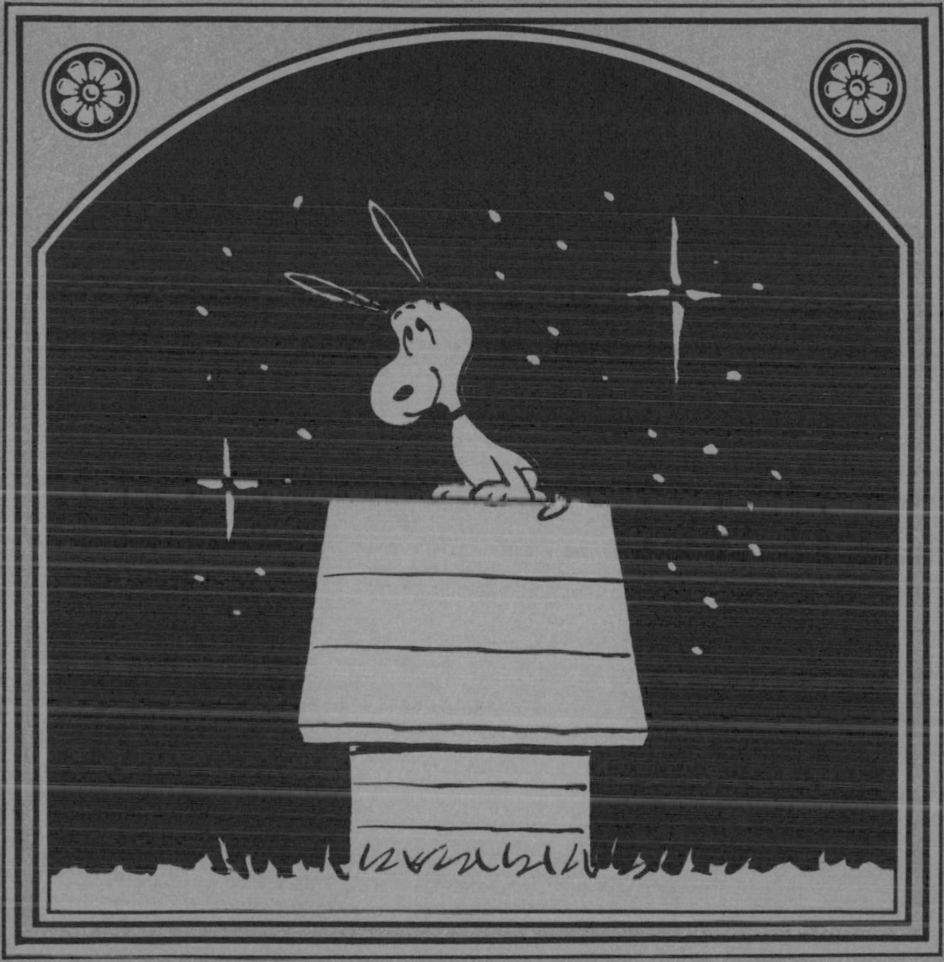

I miss Mr. Peepers.

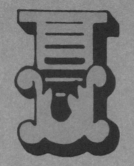

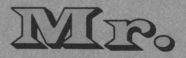

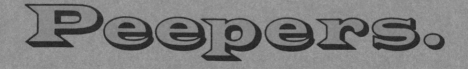

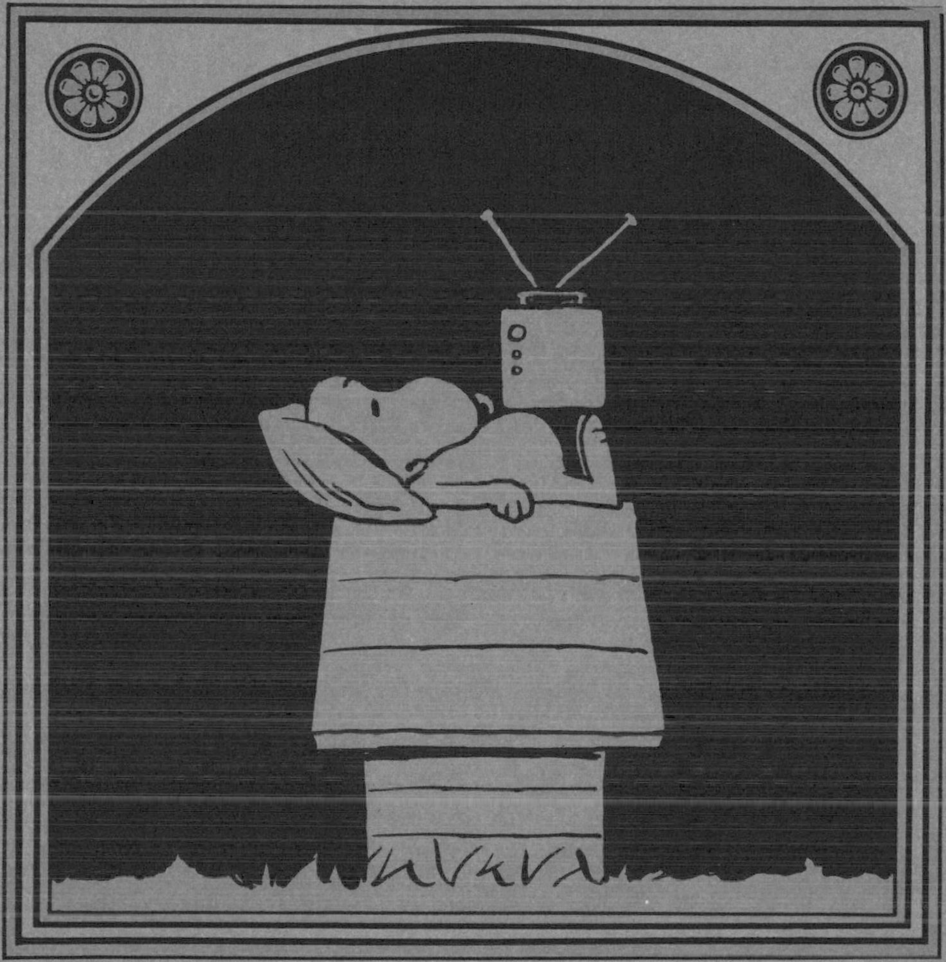

ome
guys
never really
learn
to do
anything.

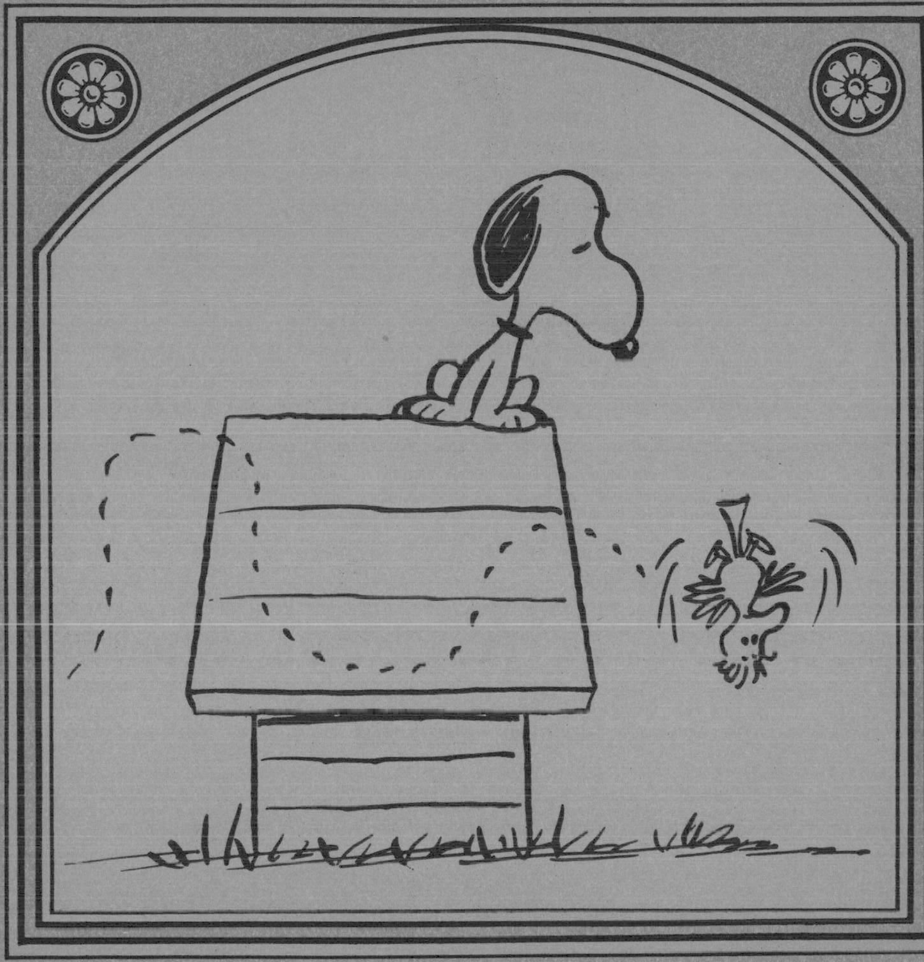

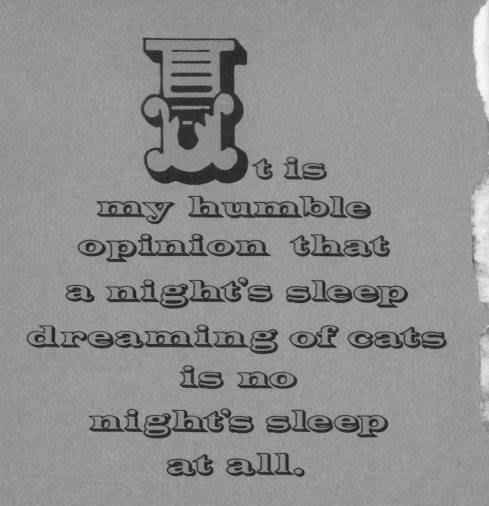

It is my humble opinion that a night's sleep dreaming of cats is no night's sleep at all.

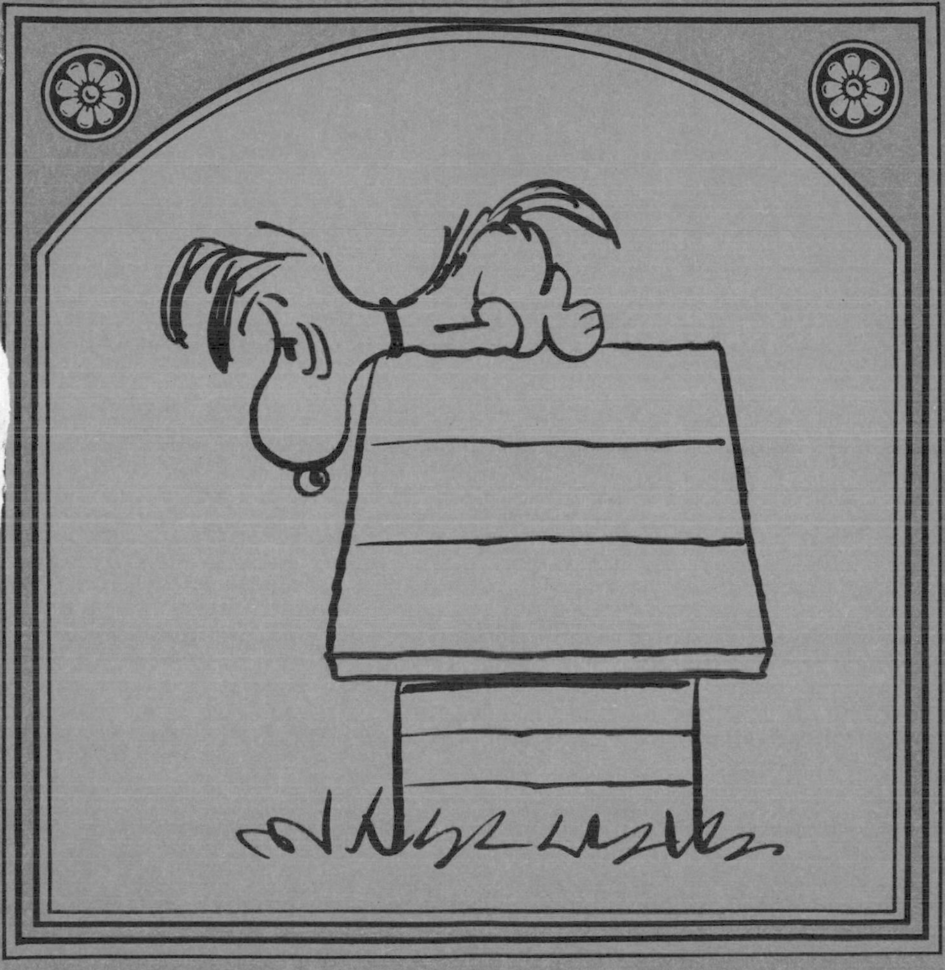

he
only time I hear
from the
Daisy Hill
Puppy Farm
Alumni Association
is when they
want another
donation!

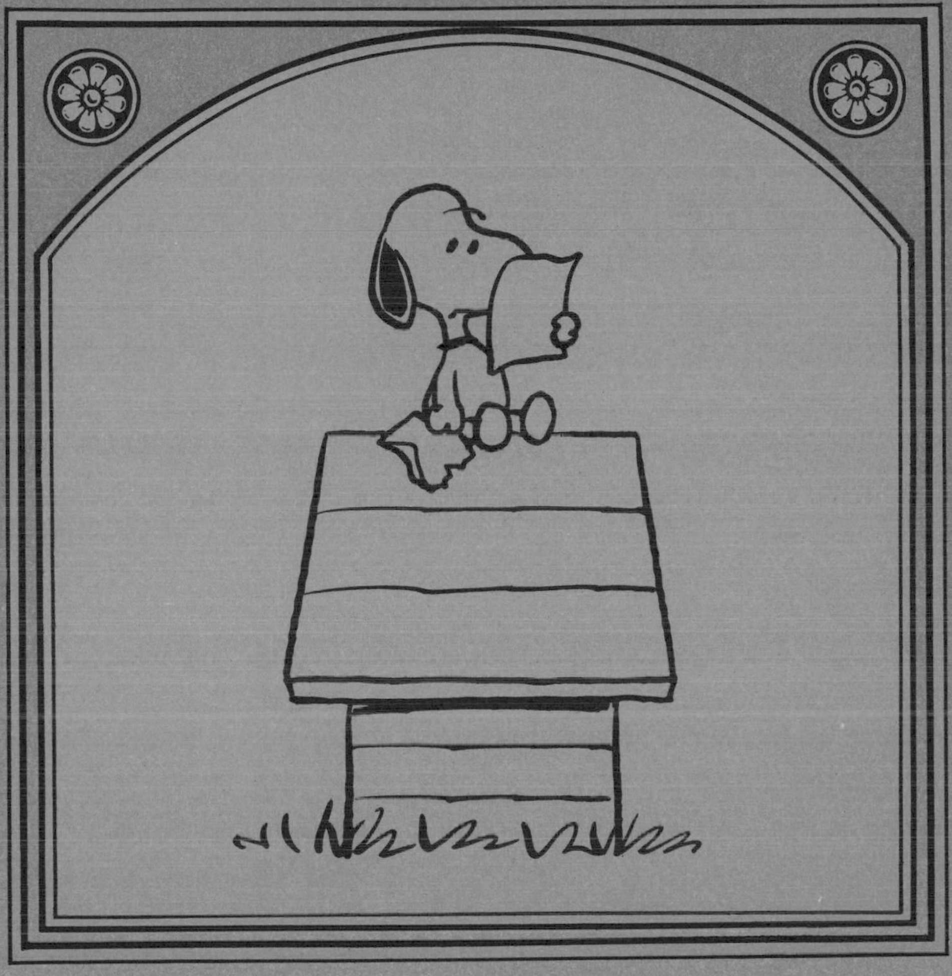

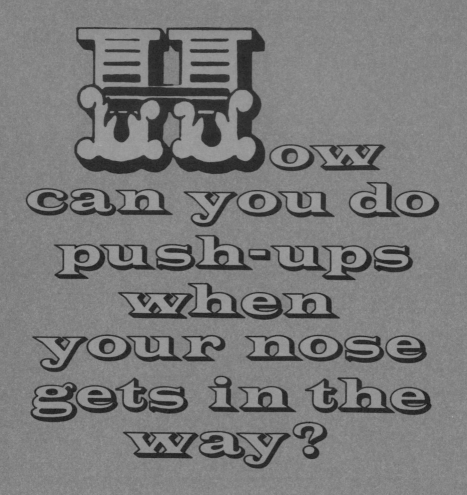

How can you do push-ups when your nose gets in the way?

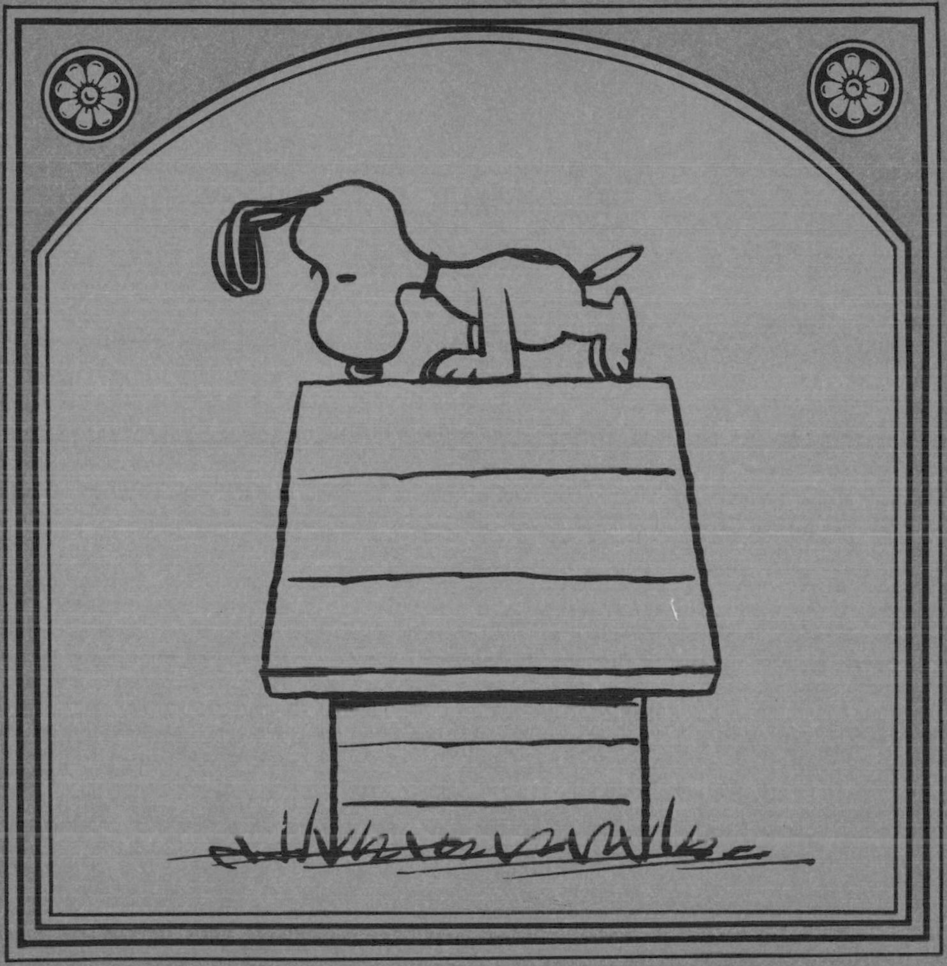

I always have a few friends over for Bridge on Thursdays.

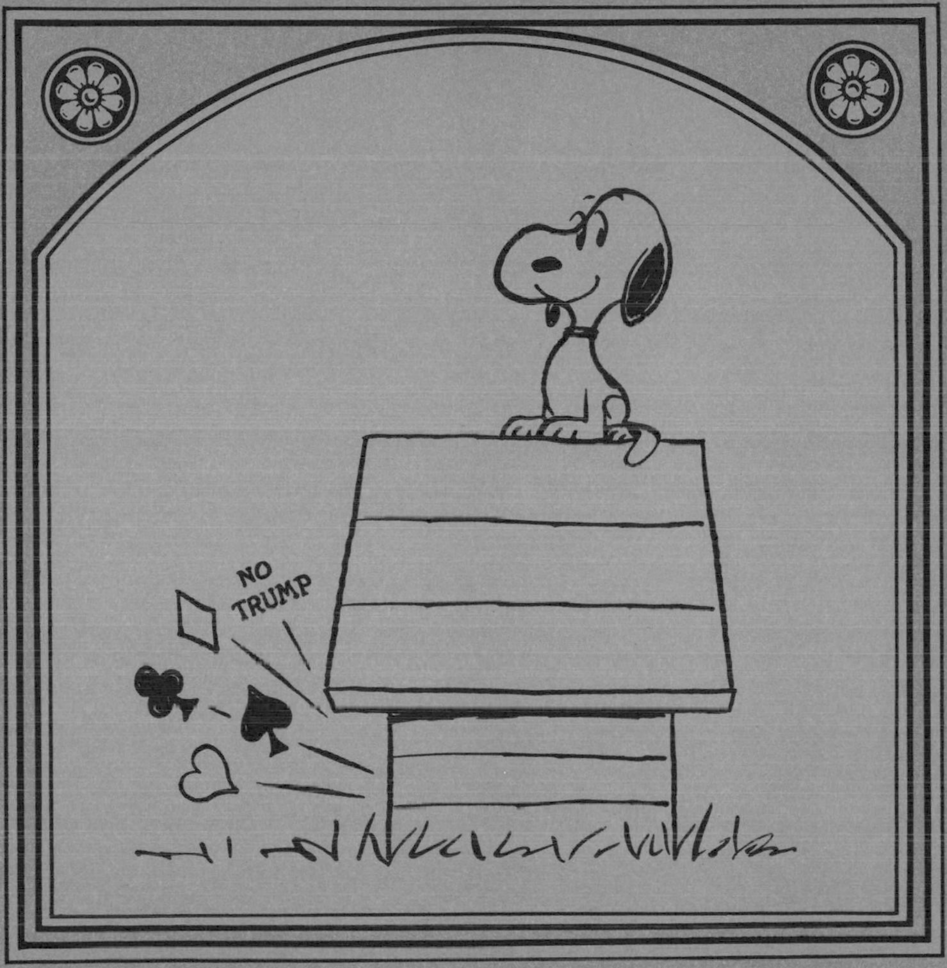
NO
TRUMP

About
five minutes
of this is
all I can
take...
then I get
claustrophobia!

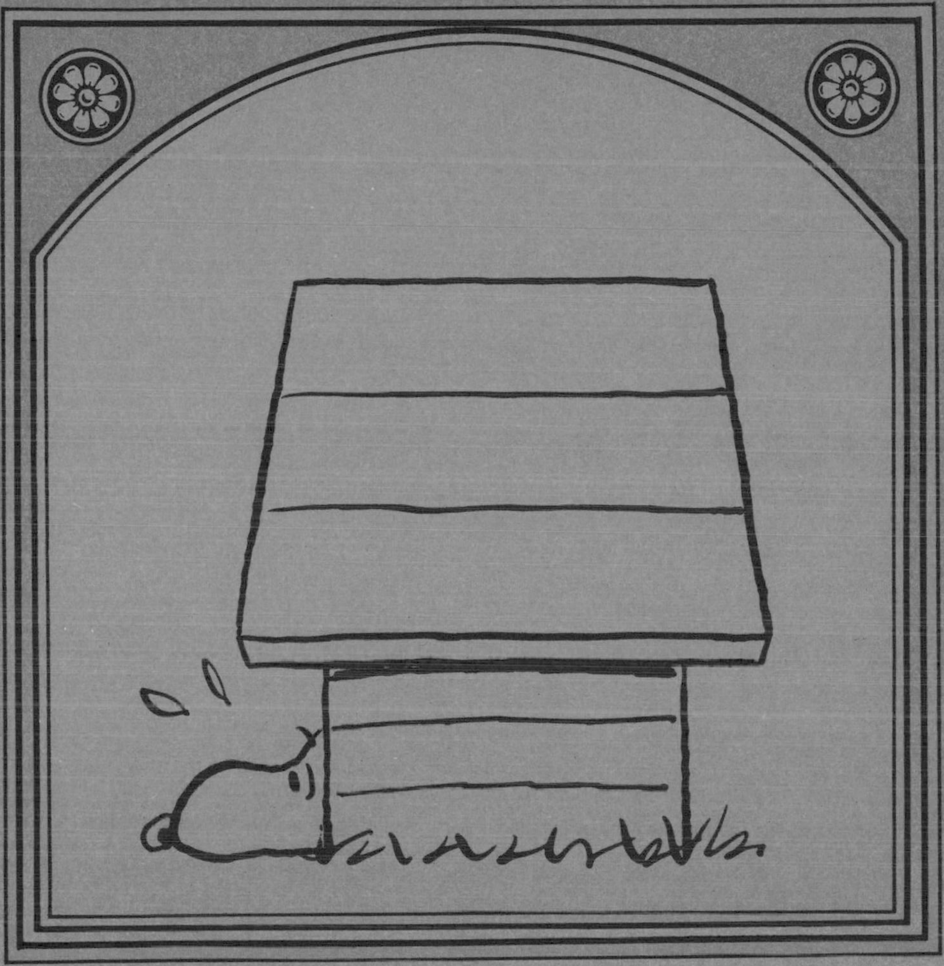

Commuter!

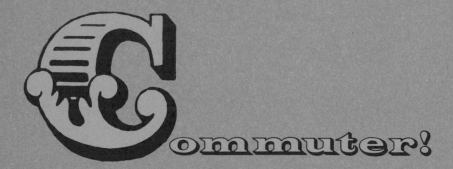

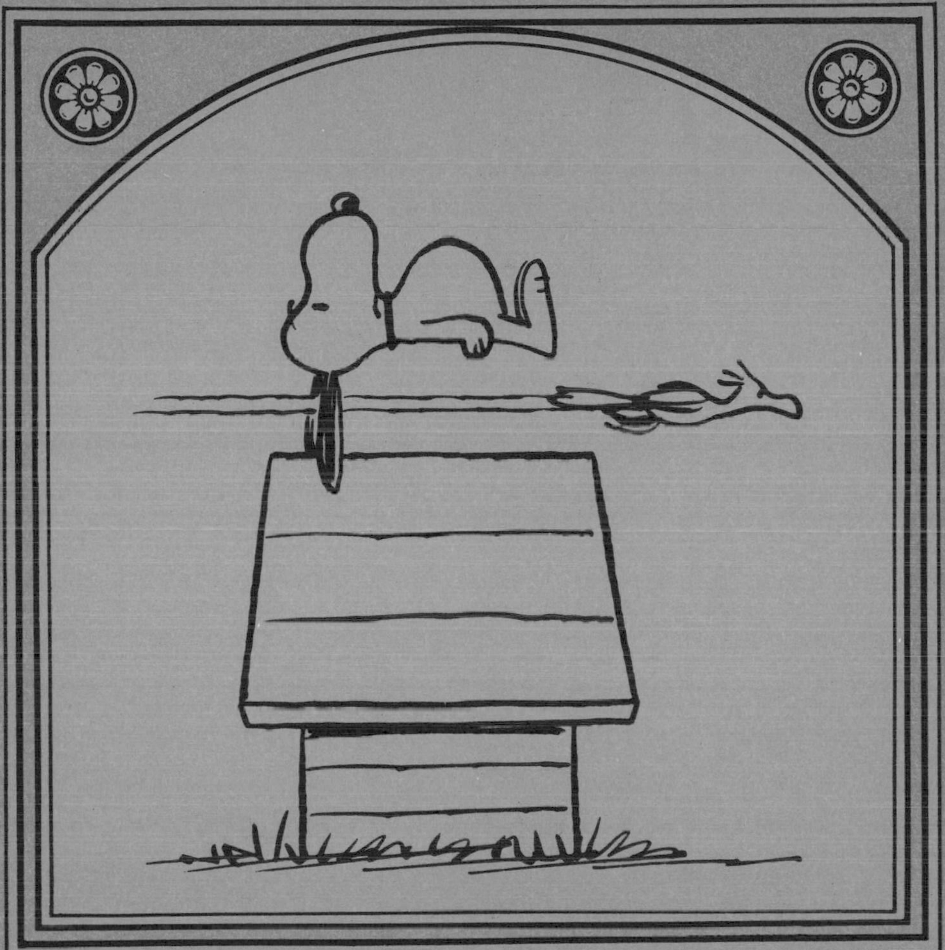

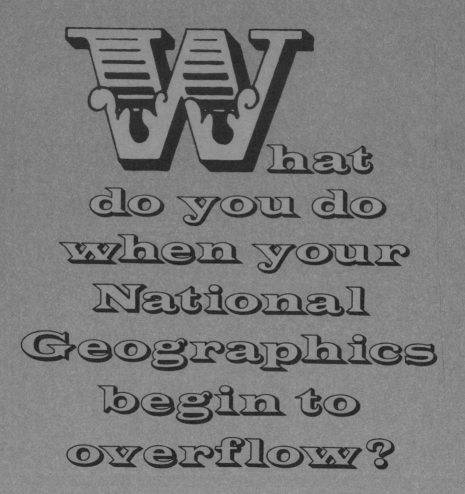

What do you do when your National Geographics begin to overflow?

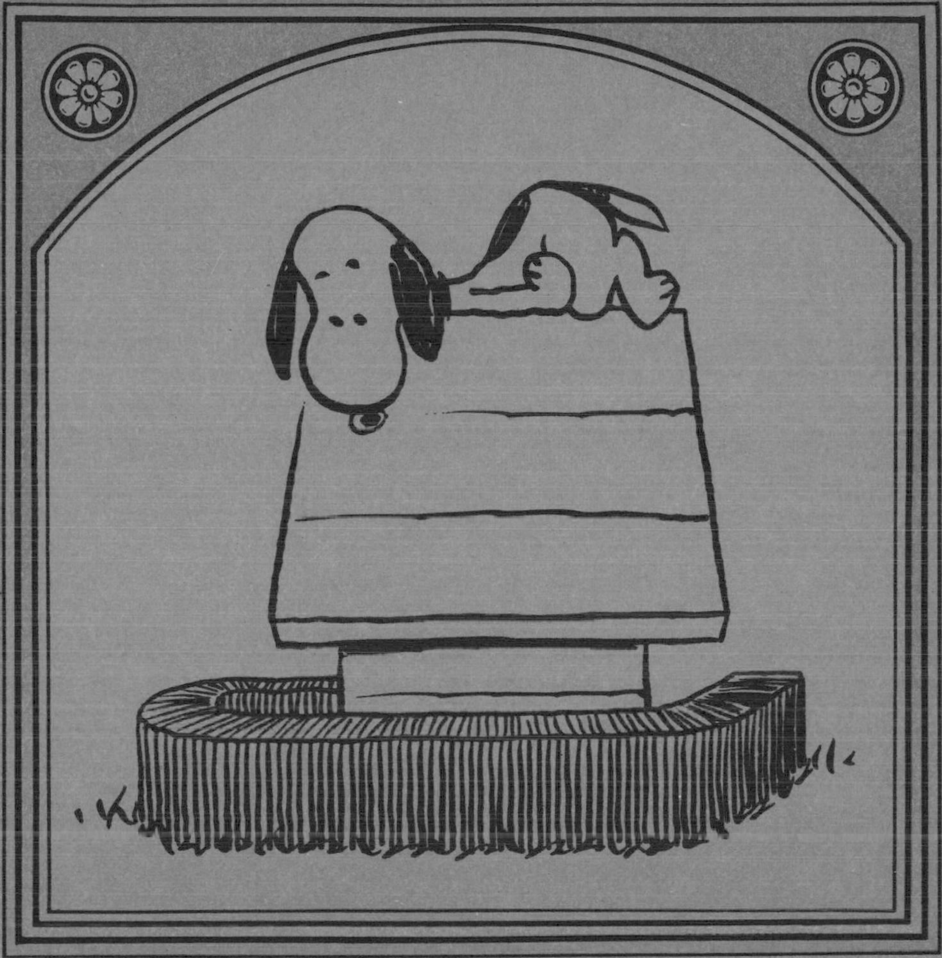

Is

it

fall

already?

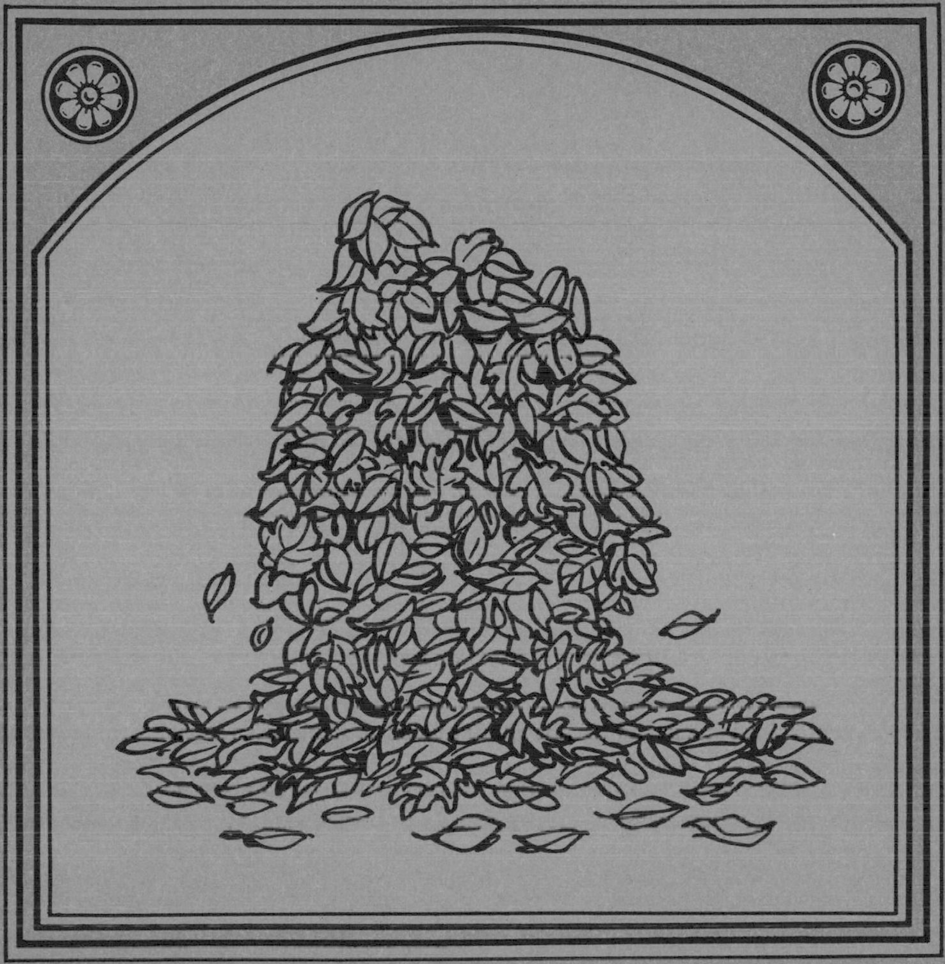

I live
in constant fear
that someone
will break in
and
steal all of my
Hank Williams
records.

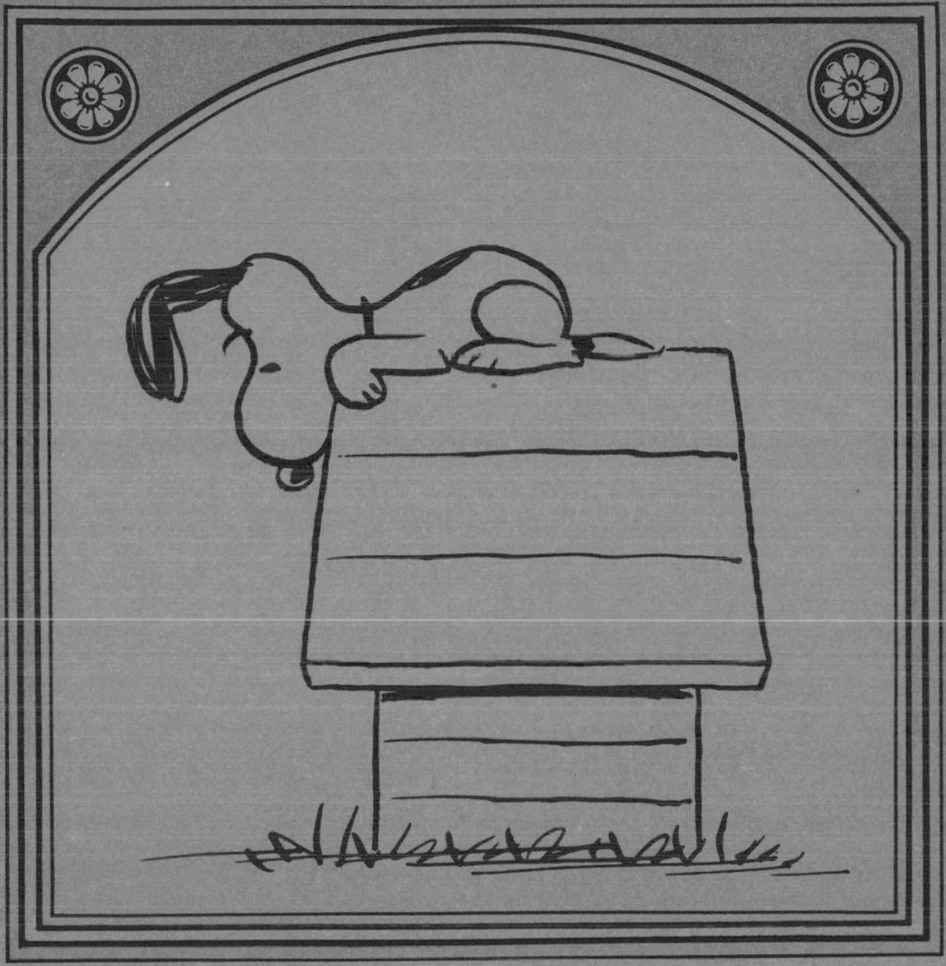

So
what's wrong
with
having
a
night
light?

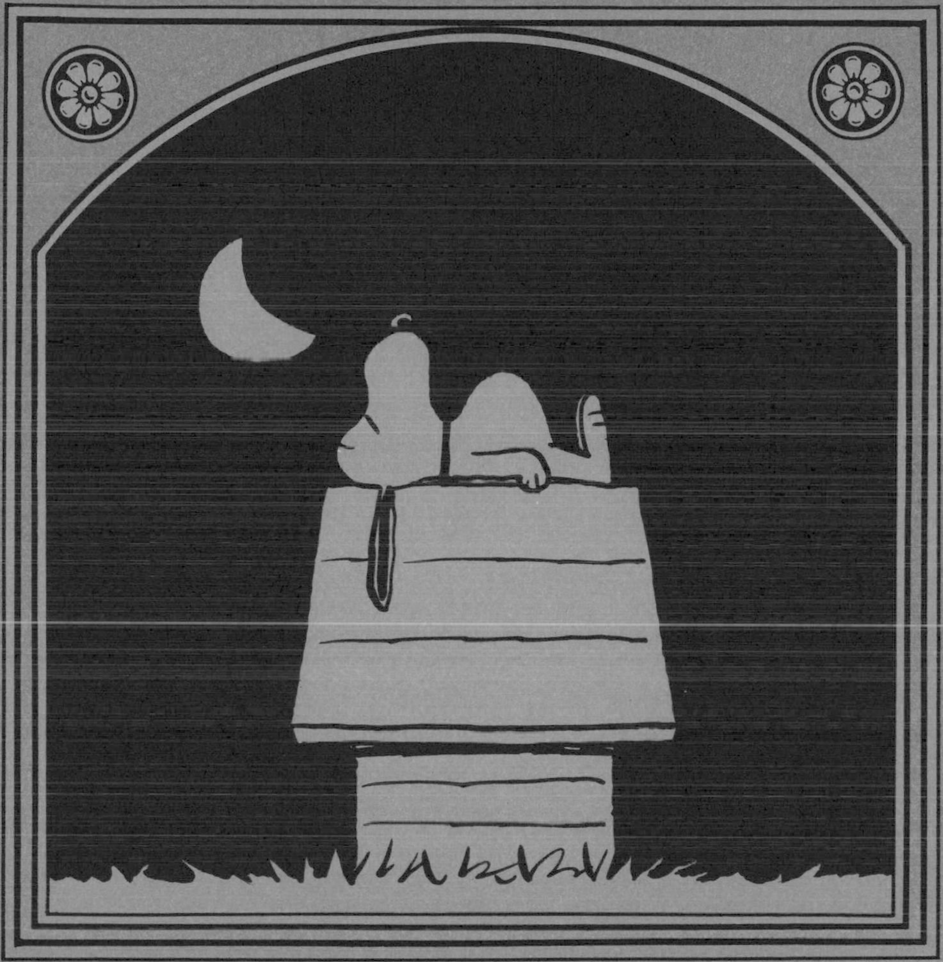

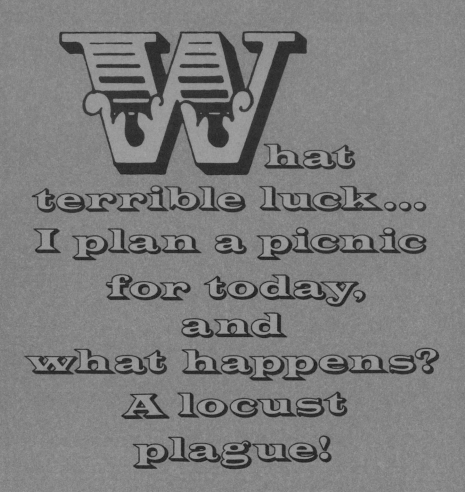

What terrible luck... I plan a picnic for today, and what happens? A locust plague!

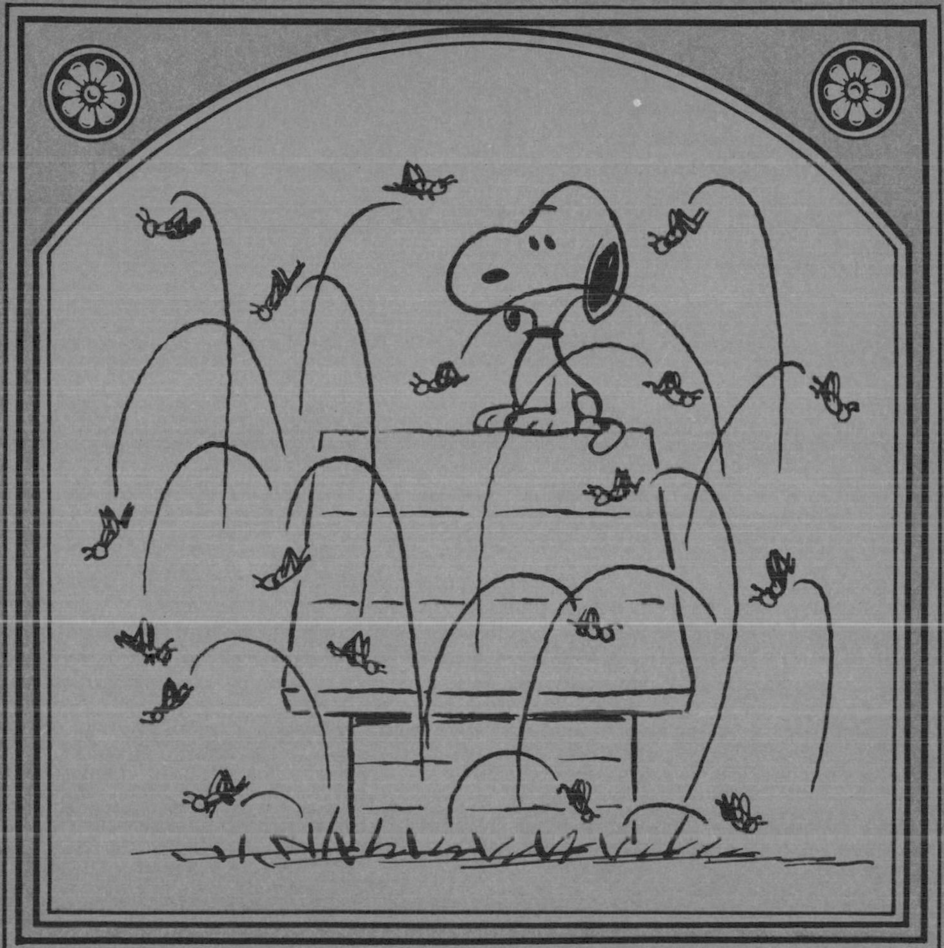

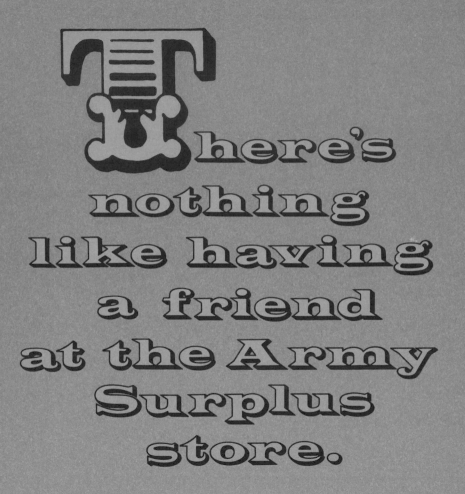

There's nothing like having a friend at the Army Surplus store.

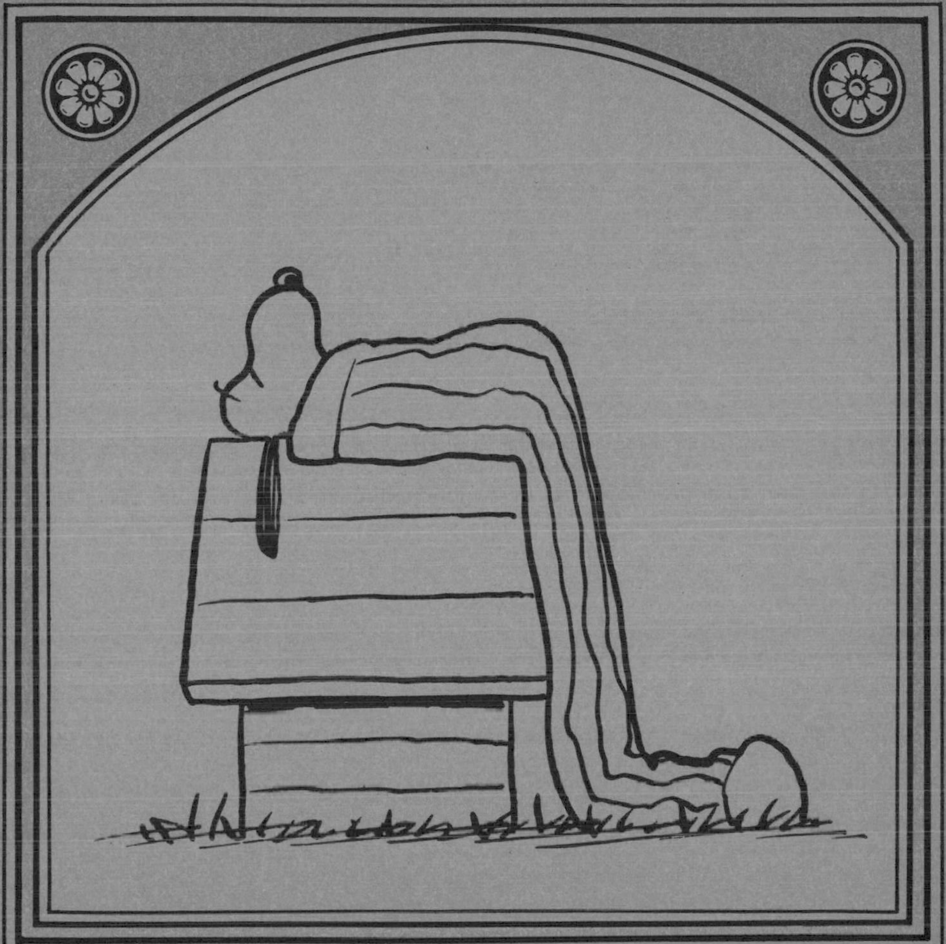

Rats! Someone left the light on over the pool table!

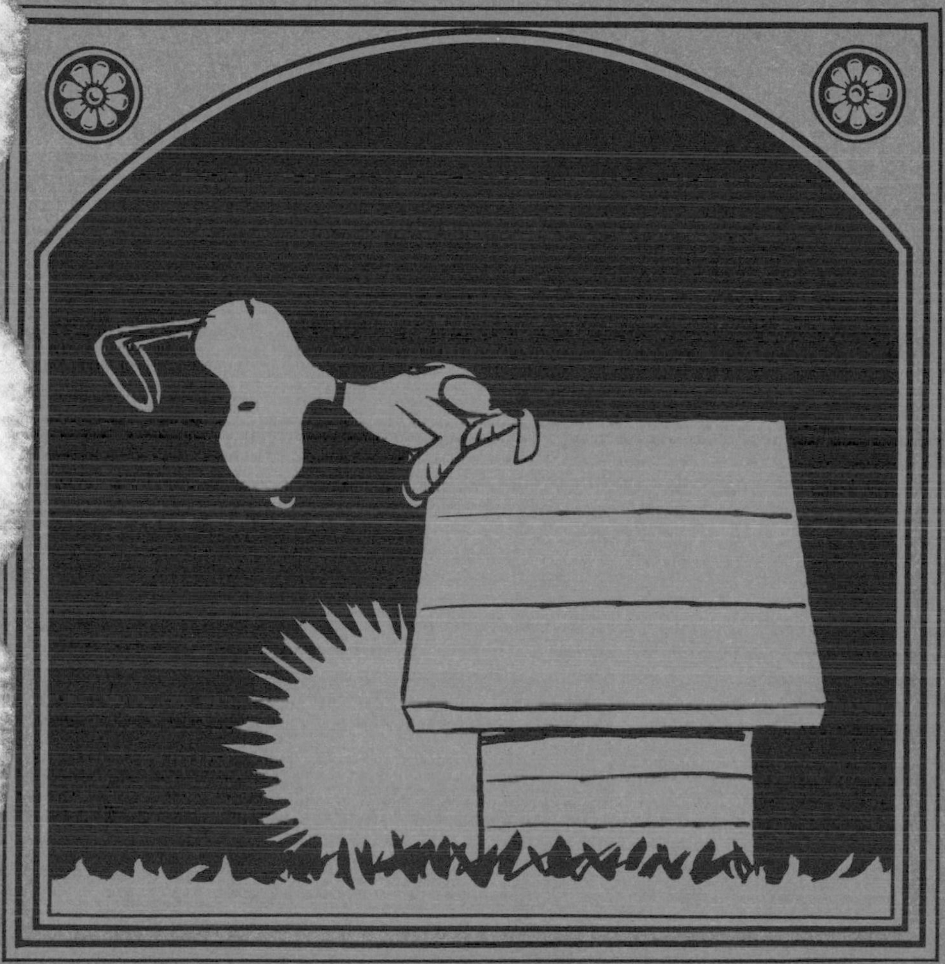

I think I'm allergic to morning.

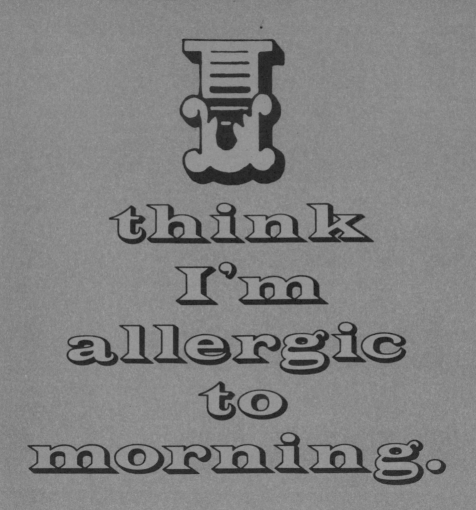

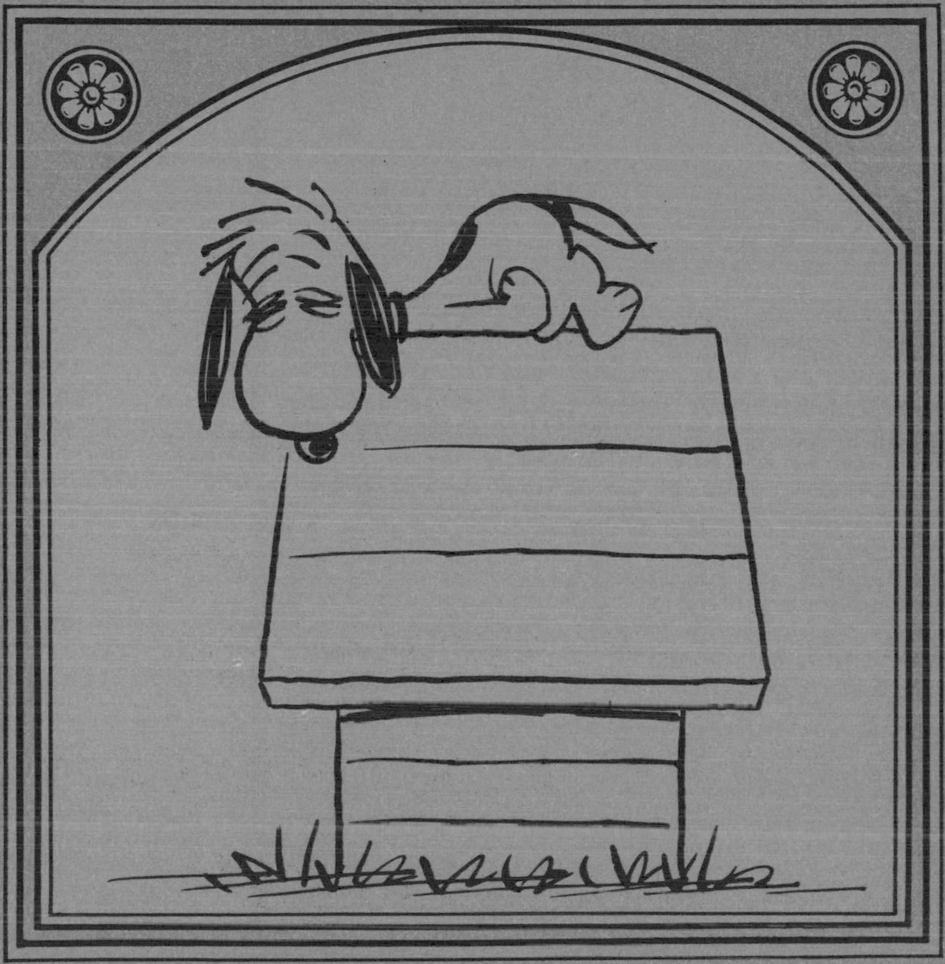

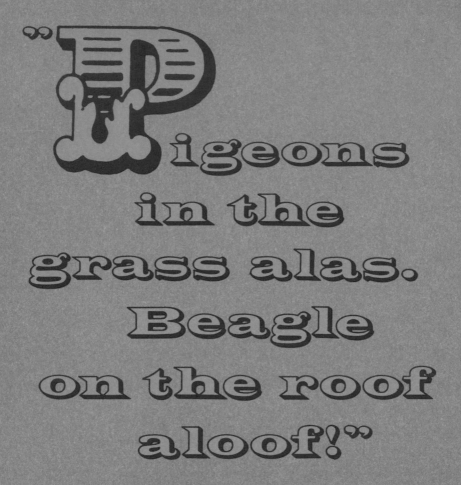

"Pigeons in the grass alas. Beagle on the roof aloof!"

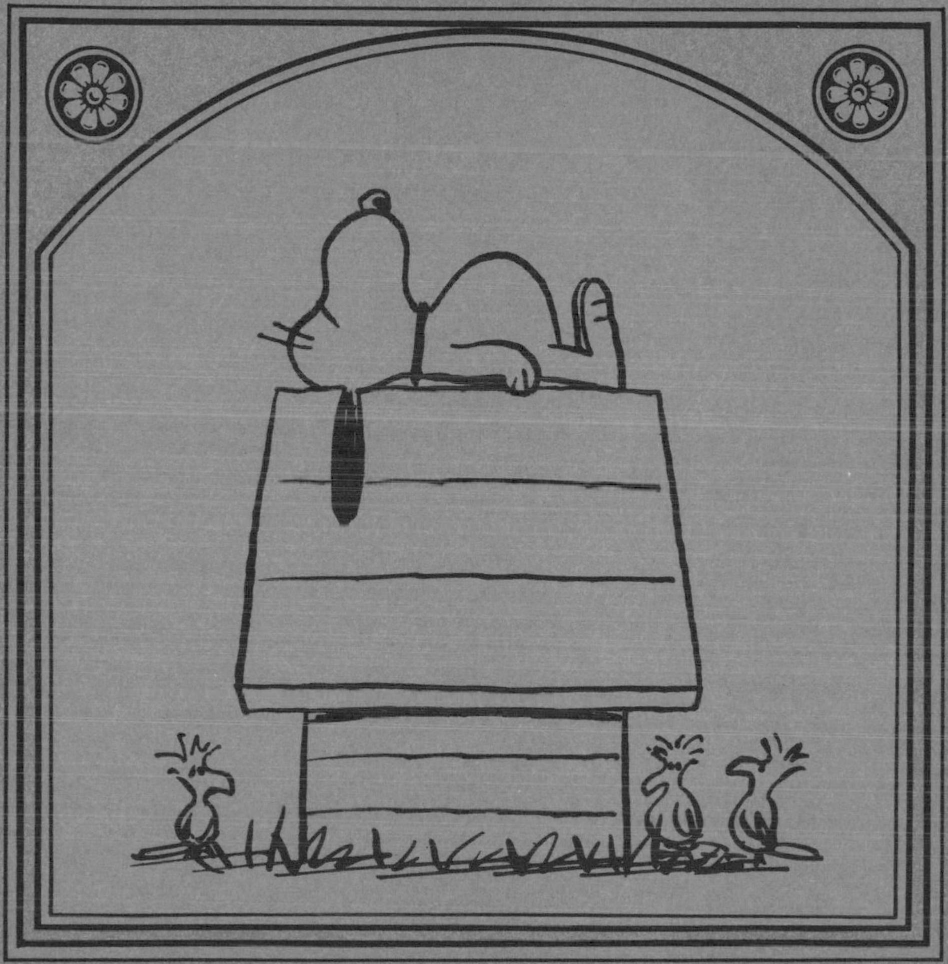

I hate windy days.

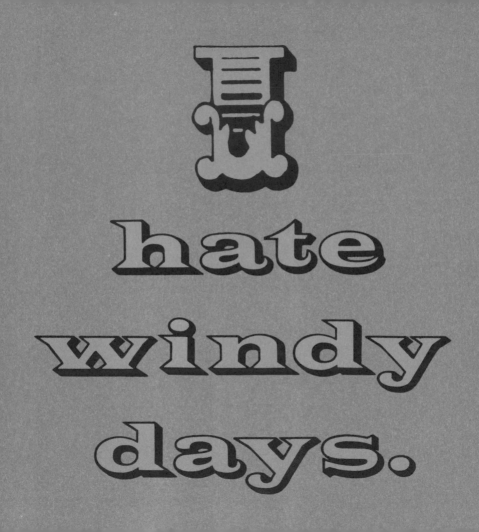

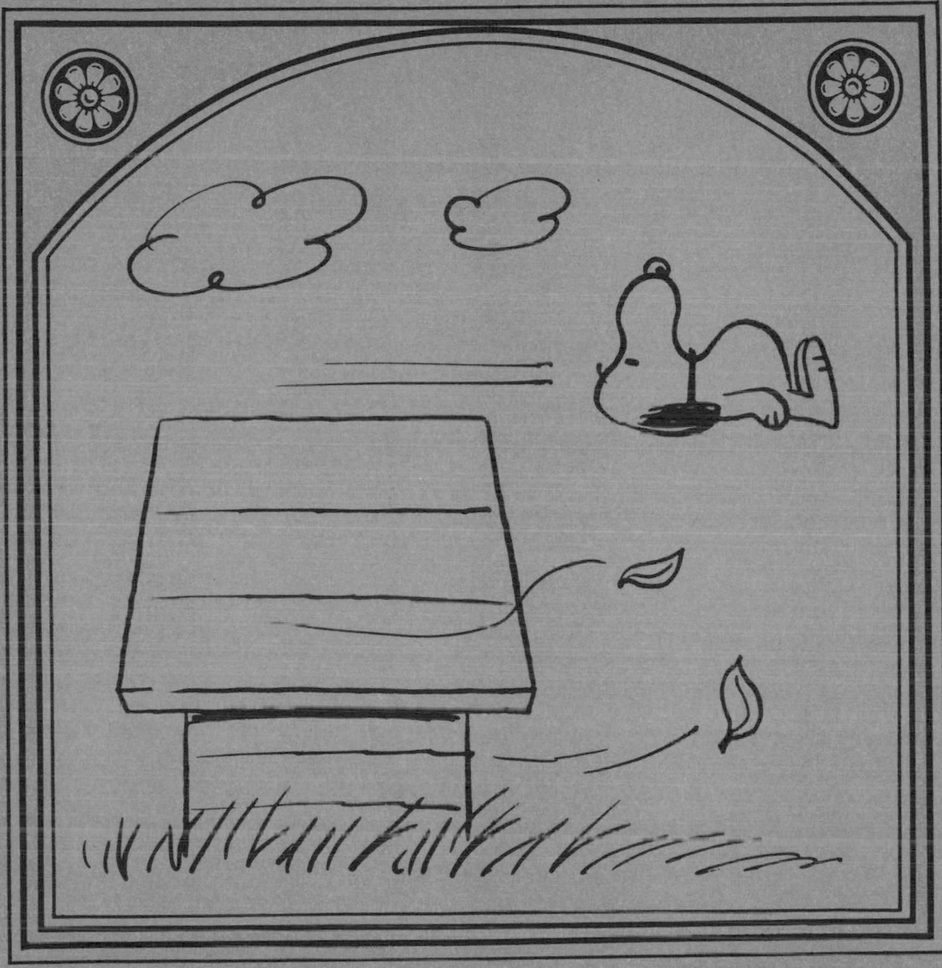

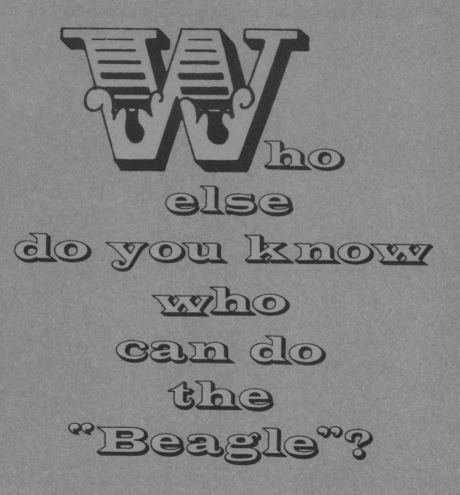

Who else do you know who can do the "Beagle"?

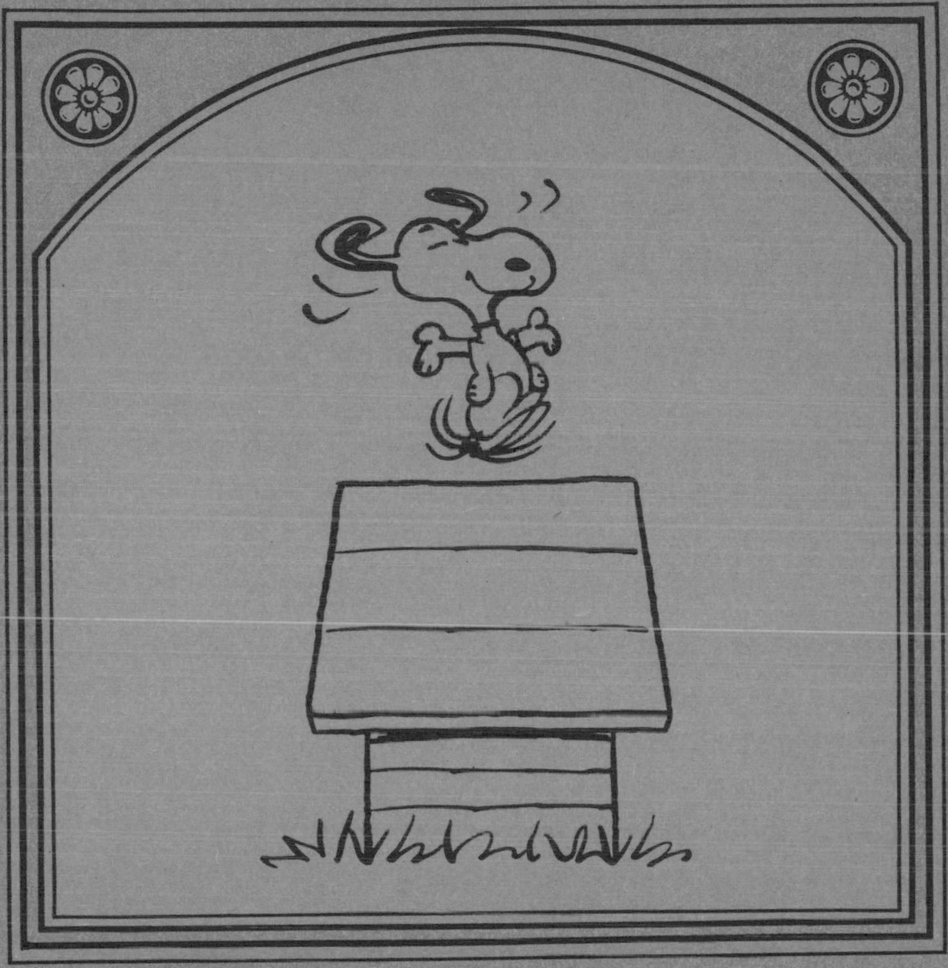

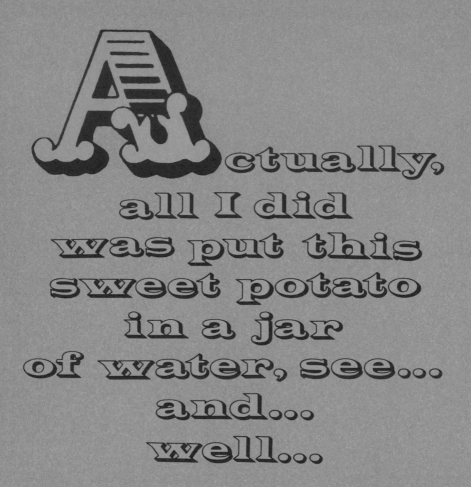

Actually, all I did was put this sweet potato in a jar of water, see... and... well...

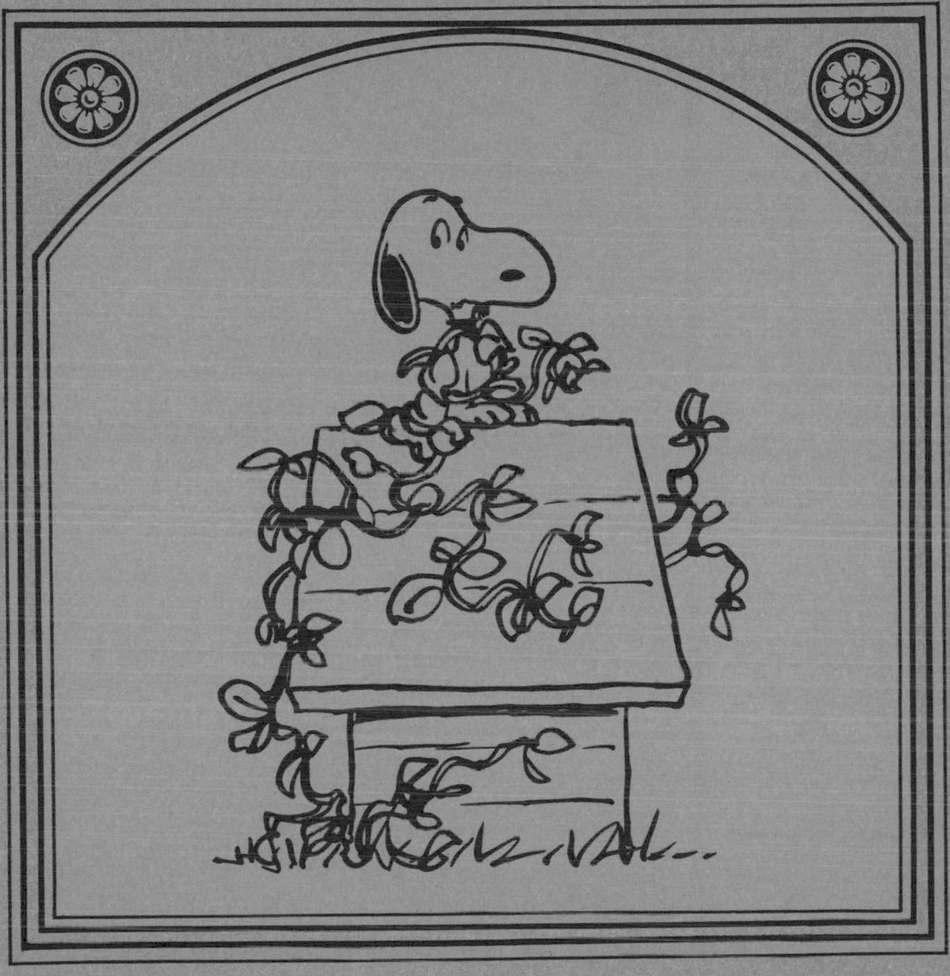

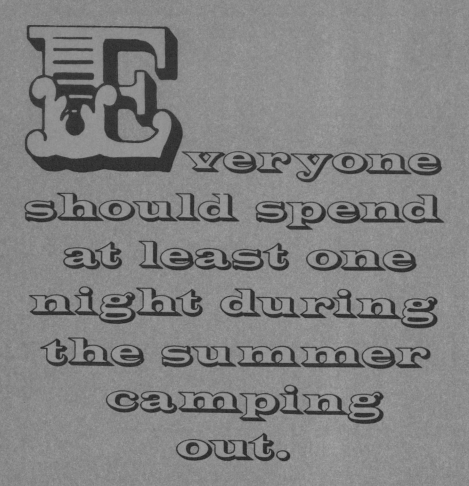

Everyone should spend at least one night during the summer camping out.

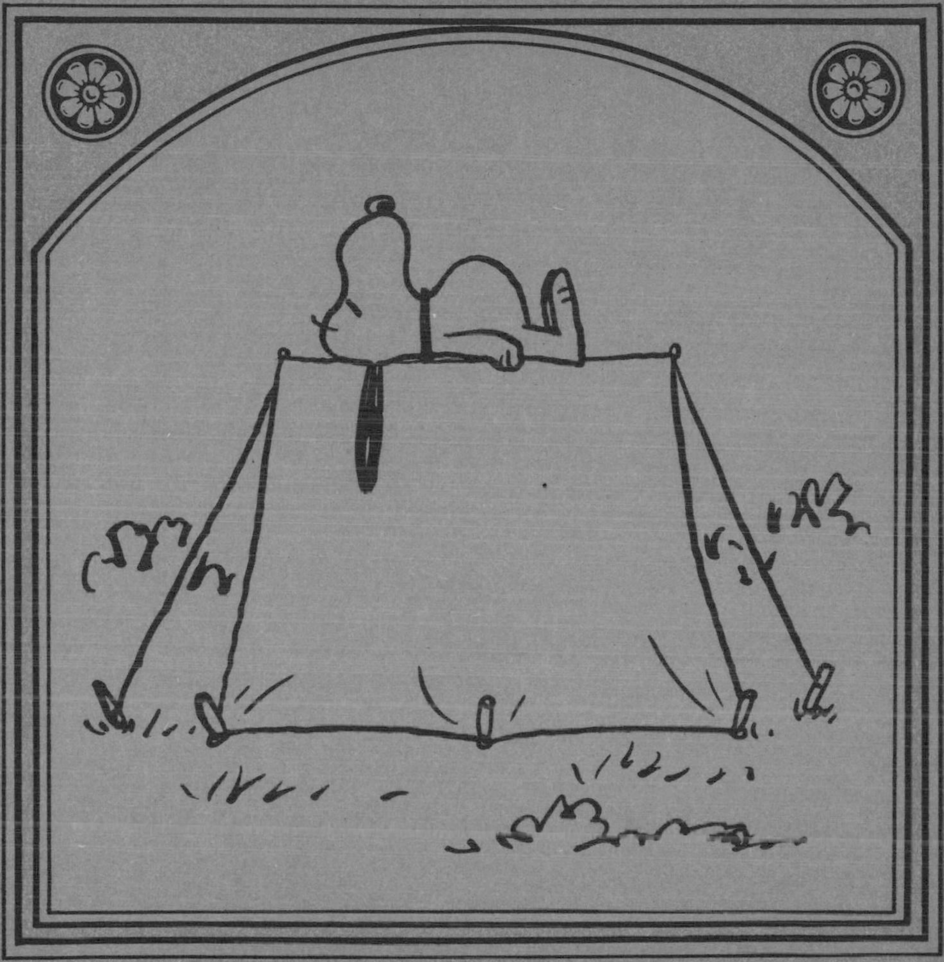

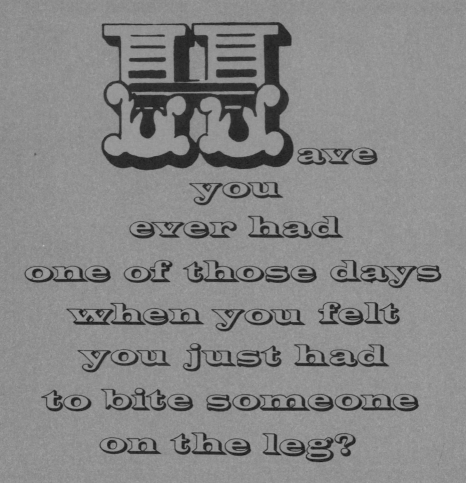

Have you ever had one of those days when you felt you just had to bite someone on the leg?

The
worst part
about living alone
is not having
someone
to bring you
tea and toast
at
bedtime.

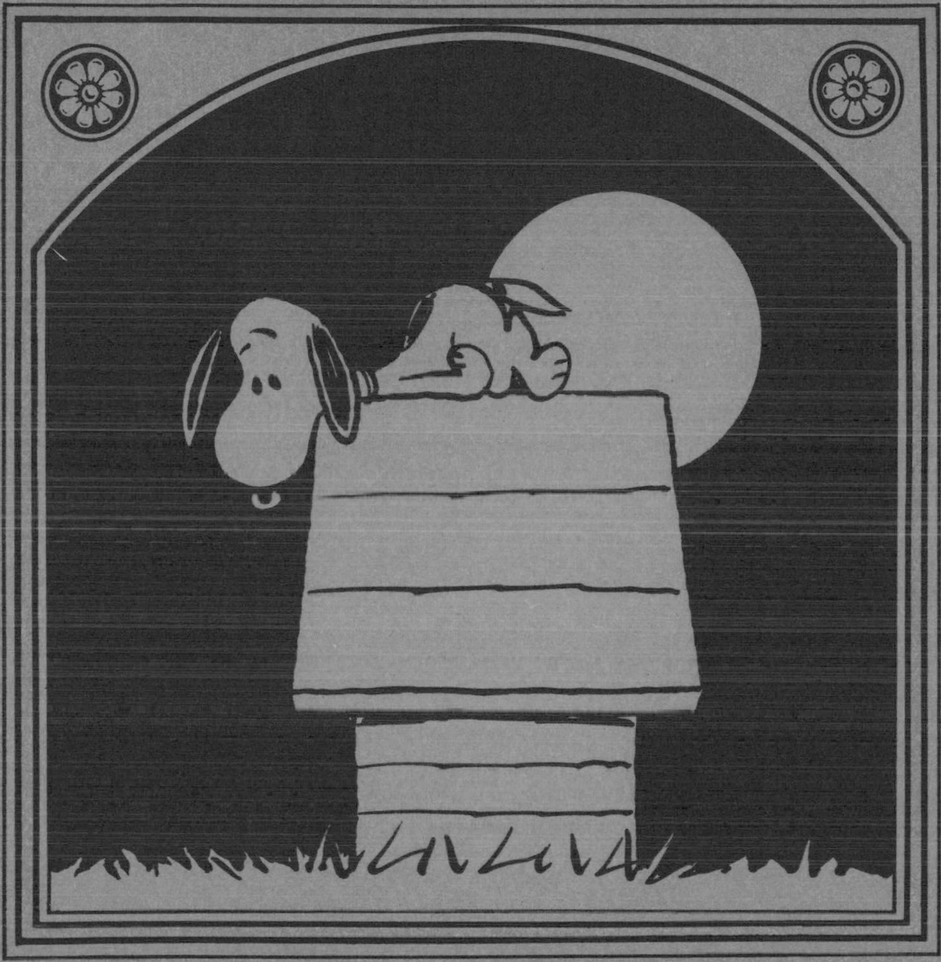

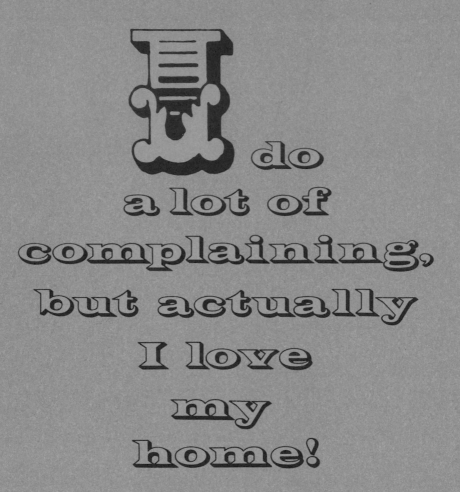

I do
a lot of
complaining,
but actually
I love
my
home!

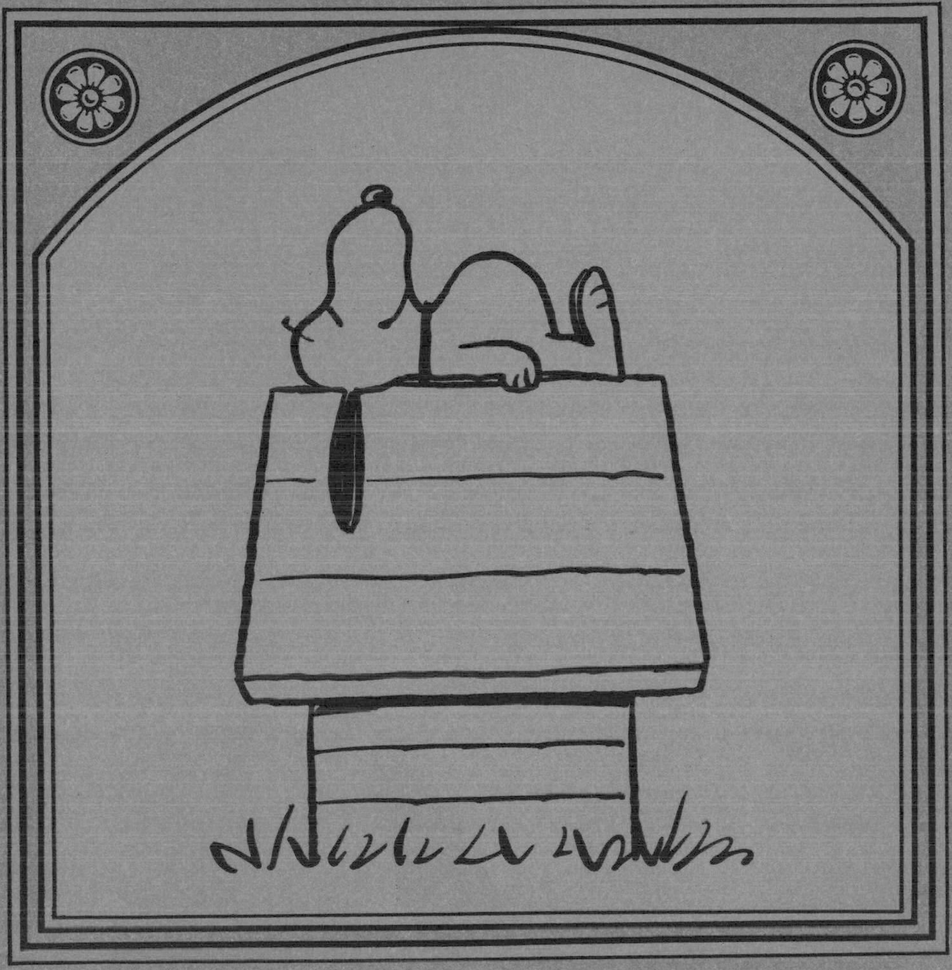

OTHER BOOKS
BY
CHARLES M. SCHULZ

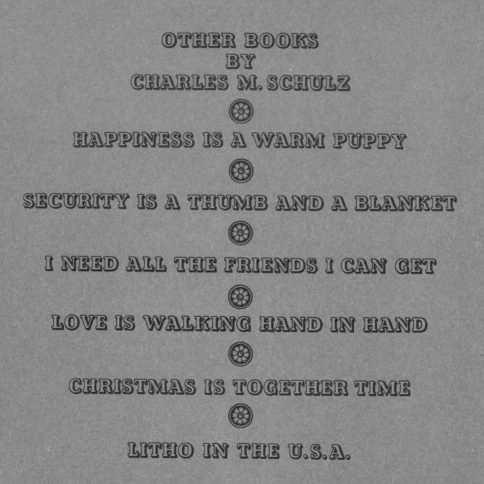

HAPPINESS IS A WARM PUPPY

SECURITY IS A THUMB AND A BLANKET

I NEED ALL THE FRIENDS I CAN GET

LOVE IS WALKING HAND IN HAND

CHRISTMAS IS TOGETHER TIME

LITHO IN THE U.S.A.